# Death and the Hereafter

## A Bible Study on How to Face Death with Confidence and Not Fear

## By Kelly Foster

**Available on Amazon**

* Eight-week Bible study.

* Designed for self-study or small groups.

* Five daily lessons are provided for each week and will take approximately 30 minutes or less to complete.

* Students are encouraged to study at their own pace.

* No required lectures.

All Scripture references are taken from English Standard Version (ESV) unless otherwise noted. Feel free to use your favorite Bible translation or the free ESV at https://www.esv.org.

# Introduction

# Lessons

## Week 1 - From Dust to Dust

## Week 2 - Planned by God

## Week 3 - No Fear in Death

## Week 4 - Your Last Breath

## Week 5 - The Soul Continues to Exist

## Week 6 - The Second Coming of Christ

## Week 7 - Righteous Judgment

## Week 8 - Declared from the Beginning

**Prayer of Repentance** - *If you do not know Jesus Christ as your personal Lord and Savior, a prayer of repentance is provided at the end of this Bible study so that you too can have assurance in death and the hereafter.......(Page 141)*

# Introduction

*Time is short. Eternity is long. It is only reasonable that this short life be lived in the light of eternity.*
Charles Spurgeon

Death is a scary thing. The uncertainty of what lies beyond the grave has haunted the masses from the beginning of time. Many hold to superstitions and fables as they attempt to understand death through human imagination and mysticism instead of the truth of God's Word.

Self-preservation is one thing we all have in common. Our natural instinct is to want to live. Even animals have a natural survival instinct. We will go through painful medical procedures and make tremendous financial and emotional sacrifices in efforts to stay alive. People will abandon their moral and spiritual beliefs to avoid death, only to learn that no matter how hard they try death is inevitable.

Ecclesiastes 3:11 tells us that God has put eternity in our hearts. Believers and unbelievers alike want to live forever. In their quest for immortality, tech giants and other billionaires are funding research in hopes that in the future a person's thinking mind can be uploaded and live in a computer long after his or her physical body has died.

Life is but a fleeting moment as death is looming over all who live. The sting of death reaches the young and the old, the rich and the poor, the powerful and the helpless. No one can escape his or her inevitable and unpredictable death.

The process of death can be horrific for some while peaceful for others. Death may come suddenly, tragically, following a long illness, or simply as the result of old age after a life well lived. With every breath, we draw closer to our last. Death is not natural to God's very good creation. Death is the result of sin and the final ending to life in this fallen world.

Scripture teaches that Christians do not need to fear death. Even at death's door, God reassures us that He is near. While we are to cherish life, death for believers is far better. Our inheritance as children of God is eternal life. No mystical powers or secret knowledge of the underworld is required. No medical miracles or computer uploads are necessary. Resurrection by the Spirit of God is the one and only avenue to life eternal.

With Jesus as our escort, we will safely and securely pass from this life into the next.

# Week 1 - From Dust to Dust

In order to study death and the hereafter, we need to first consider the origin of human life. The Bible opens with the story of creation and illustrates the importance of God's very special creation - mankind.

If you have not done so recently, read or review Genesis 1:26 thru 2:25.

1. God created mankind to be in an intimate relationship with Him.

Consider the following.

a. In whose likeness were we created (Genesis 1:26-27)?

b. What did God tell the man and woman to do (Genesis 1:28)?

c. How did God provide for their needs (Genesis 1:29)?

d. What command was given to the man and woman (Genesis 2:16-17)?

e. Why did God create Eve (Genesis 2:18)?

f. How was Eve created (Genesis 2:22)?

g. How does Adam describe his bond with Eve, and how is this bond represented in their marriage (Genesis 2:23-24)?

h. Why were Adam and Eve "not ashamed" (Genesis 2:25, also refer to Genesis 1:31)?

2. On the sixth day, God finished His creation. After looking at everything He had made, God declared it to be very good. Adam and Eve were sinless and naked. They were without the shame of sin.

How do you think their relationship with God and each other was like during this time of utopia in the Garden of Eden?

*No human being...is ever conceived outside God's will or ever conceived apart from God's image.  Life is a gift from God created in His own image.*

John F. MacArthur

## Day 2 - Image Bearers of God

3. In Genesis 1, we see similarities and differences with the creation of man vs animals. Like Adam, animals came from the earth and were given the breath of life. However, only mankind was made in the image of God, animals were not.

Children inherit their parents' physical characteristics, mannerisms, and DNA. Likewise, as God's image bearers, we were created to have His attributes. While we do share in some of God's attributes, we do not share in all of them, nor do we demonstrate any beyond a weakened or tainted version.

Incommunicable attributes are specific only to God. Examples of incommunicable attributes of God are Holiness, Immutability (does not change), Infinite (without measure or limit), Omnipresent (everywhere simultaneously), Omniscience (perfect, complete knowledge), and Self-existent (not dependent).

Can you think of any others?

4. Attributes of God that are also shared by humans are called communicable attributes.

Several communicable attributes of God are listed below. How is our capacity for these attributes different when compared to God?

a. Love

b. Emotion

c. Justice

d. Creativity

e. Reason (think logically)

f. Forgiveness

g. Can you think of any other characteristics that humans share with God?

6. By creating us in His own image we are able to better understand our Creator. God gives us illustrations to teach us about Himself. For example, the Trinity - the Father, the Son and the Holy Spirit teach us about different roles and responsibilities in a family relationship.

Consider the examples provided in Ephesians 5:25, 1 Corinthians 11:3 and John 14:31.

Why do you think God chose to create us in His image?

*It is not just that we exist and God has always existed, it is also that God necessarily exists in an infinitely better, stronger, more excellent way. The difference between God's being and ours is more than the difference between the sun and a candle, more than the difference between the ocean and a raindrop... God's being is qualitatively different.*

Wayne Grudem

6. Adam and Eve were created in God's likeness and with His characteristics such as creativity, emotion, and intellect along with the ability to make moral and ethical decisions. As such, they had free will to choose to obey God or rebel against Him.

Read Genesis 3.

a. How did the serpent deceive Eve (v 4-5)?

b. What enticed her to eat from the tree of the knowledge of good and evil (v 6)?

c. How was Adam prompted to eat the forbidden fruit (v 6)?

d. Adam and Eve disobeyed God when they ate the forbidden fruit.

What immediately happened after their sin of disobedience and rebellion (v 7)?

e. God loved Adam and Eve and would walk with them in the cool of the day.

When God came to visit, why did they hide (vs 8-10)?

What did their sin expose?

7. In Genesis 3, we learn that Satan appeared in the Garden as a serpent and deceived Eve. In verses 4-5, the serpent said to the woman, "You will not surely die. For God knows that when you eat of it your eyes will be opened, and you will be like God, knowing good and evil."

Satan tells Eve to doubt God's Word and implies that God is trying to hide valuable knowledge and power that would make her like God. Eve believed Satan's lies, ate the forbidden fruit of the tree of the knowledge of good and evil, and gave some to Adam which he ate.

The Fall occurred when Adam and Eve disobeyed God. The serpent, Adam, and Eve received judgments for their rebellion.

What final judgment was placed on Adam for his sin in verse 19?

8. Adam and Eve should have trusted God at His Word. He would have given them all the knowledge they would ever need. God was not trying to deceive or hide something of value from them. He was protecting Adam and Eve from corruption and death.

The serpent, on the other hand, kept his motives hidden as he lured Eve away from God by tempting her with the deceptive beauty of evil.

Read Romans 16:19.

a. What knowledge should we seek and what knowledge should we avoid?

b. How does the knowledge we seek demonstrate our trust in God?

*You are free to choose. You are not free not to choose. No choice is a choice. You are free to choose but you are not free to choose the consequences of that choice.*

Adrian Rogers

## Day 4 - The Purpose of Tests

9. God did not place the tree of the knowledge of good and evil in the garden to tempt Adam and Eve. While God does test us, He does not tempt people to sin. The forbidden tree provided opportunity for free will: obey God or not. Without options, there would be no free will for Adam and Eve.

The test of the forbidden tree revealed Adam and Eve's lack of devotion to God. Likewise, trials and tests in our lives reveal to whom or what we are devoted. Our weaknesses are exposed as we learn to walk according to God's will. Trials, tests and temptations either draw us closer to God or further away.

a. Read James 1:12-15.

What causes us to be tempted?

b. Read Psalm 26:2, Isaiah 48:10 and Zechariah 13:9.

Silver and gold are purified by fire.

What does God use to refine us as He teaches us to be like Christ?

c. Read James 1:2-4 (ESV).  Testing of our faith produces steadfastness

that we may be _____ and _____,

lacking _____.


d.  Read 1 Peter 1:6-9.


Why are trials necessary and beneficial for us?


10.  In the Garden of Eden, the devil declared war on God's very special
creation - humanity.  Satan's war continues to rage on and has intensified
since he knows his time is short (Revelation 12:12).  In order to form a line
of defense, it is important to recognize the enemy and be able to identify his
war tactics.

What do the following verses teach us about our enemy and how to defeat
him?

a.  Ephesians 6:10-11

b. James 4:7-8

c. 1 Peter 5:8-9

11. Jesus demonstrated how to resist the devil. When tempted in the wilderness, Jesus overcame Satan's attacks with Scripture (Matthew 4:1-11).

Before His death, Jesus was in great turmoil as He knew the pain and suffering that He would soon face on the cross. Jesus fell on His face before His Father and prayed with tears and much anguish as He submitted to His Father's will (Matthew 26:36-46 and Hebrews 5:7).

Jesus demonstrated how to defeat the enemy through Scripture, prayer and obedience to God's will.

a. Read Hebrews 2:18.

How does Jesus' sufferings while He was on earth help us?

b. Read 1 Corinthians 10:12-13.

How does God help us in our times of weakness?

*The difficulties we face originate from one of three sources. Some are sent to us by the Lord to test our faith, others are the result of Satan's attacks, and still others are due to our own sinful choices.*

Charles Stanley

12.  Adam and Eve were banished from the Garden in order to prevent them from eating from the tree of life, which would have doomed them for all eternity in a permanent state of sin, death and alienation from God.  God had a better plan, a plan of redemption that began soon after they left the Garden.

Read Genesis 3:22-24.

How did God demonstrate His mercy when He banned Adam and Eve from the Garden?

13.  Every human being is a descendent of Adam and Eve.  We are all part of the same human race.

Read Romans 5:12.

What do all people inherit from Adam?

14. As a result of sin, Adam and Eve's bodies began aging, and they eventually died. In Genesis 5:5, we learn that Adam was 930 when he died.

Based on Genesis 3:19, what happened to Adam's body when he died?

15. In Genesis 2:7, we learned that God formed Adam from small particles (dust) from the earth, breathed into his nostrils the breath of life, and Adam became a living being.

Read Job 34:14-15.

What would happen to all mankind if God withdrew His "breath?"

16. In this first week, we've learned that humanity is very special to the Creator. God created us to be like Him. He loves us; therefore, He pursues an intimate relationship with us.

Sin is a choice with dire consequences; sin separates us from our loving Creator. Scripture instructs us to examine our hearts and minds and identify areas of temptation and rebellion that draw us away from God. As Adrian Rogers said, "We are sinners by birth, by nature, by choice, and by practice." We are all sinners, and we must accept that basic reality in order to undeniably understand our need for a Savior.

Read Lamentations 3:40.

What should we do if sin is hindering our relationship with God?

*When you live in the light of eternity, your values change.*

Rick Warren

# Week 2 - Planned by God

1. God did not create mankind because He was lonely. He did not have a void that required human interaction. God is self-sufficient. He is and always has been perfectly happy and perfectly content. God the Father, God the Son, and God the Holy Spirit were not lonely. Nor does God need anything.

The following passages help us understand why God created humans.

a. Read Acts 17:24-25.

Does God need anything from humans? In other words, does God lack something that only humans can provide?

If no, why not?

b. Read Colossians 1:16.

All things were created through Him and _____.

c. Revelation 4:11.

What is the reason given for the existence and creation of all things?

2. Since God knows the future, He knew beforehand that Adam and Eve and their descendants would sin and rebel against Him. Holy God knew from eternity passed that sin would ruin His relationship with His creation. God knew before He created us that He would also have to become one of us, and die for our sins, so that we could have eternal life with Him.

God created us in His image, then He was made in our image (Jesus Christ) in order to reconcile us back to Himself (Philippians 2:5-11).

What do the following passages reveal about the eternal (family) relationship God is developing with those who believe in Him?

a. Isaiah 54:5

b. Revelation 21:9

c. 2 Corinthians 11:2

d. Ephesians 5:25-32

3. Read Psalm 8.

Today's lesson leads us to ask the same question as David who was in awe of God's majesty and His love for His creation, "what is man that you are mindful of him?" (v 4).

How does this Psalm inspire you?

We were created by God and for Him, for His purpose and for His pleasure. We were created in His image as His offspring. God created us because He loves us. He demonstrates His love for us by developing an intimate, loving relationship with us that will endure forever.

*God does not need us or the rest of creation for anything, yet we and the rest of creation can glorify Him and bring Him joy.*

Wayne Grudem

4. Christians understand that life has a greater mission than merely focusing on self-preservation. Our view of life and death is more purposeful and resolute than the view held by unbelievers.

Earthly pursuits have their purpose but are of little value in light of eternity. Pleasures, fame and possessions should never be our chief focus. Life has more to offer than superficial goals and self-centered aspirations.

In Ecclesiastes, Solomon, the wisest man on earth, ponders the purpose of life. He writes about the vanity of life and pleasures, wisdom and folly, and labor and rewards. Man does not always know the best route to take since we have limited wisdom in this life and no knowledge of what happens on earth after we are dead.

Read Ecclesiastes 3:1, 3:9-15 and 3:22.

a. What has God put in every person's heart so that we would look beyond this life even though we cannot fully understand all life's mysteries (v 11)?

b. What should we do and rejoice in while on earth (vs 12-13 and 22)?

c. Our earthly endeavors are temporal. God's works will last forever. What is the purpose of God's works (v 14-15)?

5. After pondering the meaning of life, Solomon provides us his conclusion.

Read Ecclesiastes 12:13-14.

In light of these verses, how should we live?

6. Worldly achievements and self-preservation should not be our primary goals in life. Solomon wisely concluded that faithfulness to God should be our focus.

We are faithful to God, when we learn to trust God more than we trust ourselves and others.

Fill in the blank. Faithfulness to God is more important than my

_____.

God is more concerned with our faithfulness to Him than our desires, possessions or success. Everything we own, see or want in this world is temporal and should be treated as such. If we aspire to have a prosperous life, we must live with an eternal focus. For believers, our reward comes after death and can only be achieved through a life that is dedicated to things that are eternal.

*When you seek God first in your daily pursuits, He promises to add unto you those things which you were pursuing (as long as they are in His will). Placing Him first in your life should be your daily goal, the main pursuit in the midst of all your other pursuits.*

Paul Chappell

8. God planned our lives before the beginning of Creation. In His eternal knowledge, He predetermined when, where and to whom we would be born. He fashioned our appearance, personalities, talents and skillsets. God was not surprised when you were born, nor will He be surprised when you die.

Read Psalm 139:1-18.

This Psalm was written by David and discusses God's involvement in his life. Similarly, God is involved in your life.

a. When did God plan to create you?

b. How well does God know you?

c. In verse 16, what was written beforehand (predetermined) in God's book?

Likewise, when we are resurrected from the dead it will be for the eternal glory of God.

We can have peace in knowing that God will work everything out for our eternal good. Whether our prayers are answered to our liking or not, God's will be done. No one or no circumstance can thwart God's perfect, eternal plan.

We pray because the All-Powerful, immeasurable God of the universe without limitation hears our prayers, responds to our needs and directs our lives in accordance with His good will.

*Prayer lays hold of God's plan and becomes the link between His will and its accomplishment on earth. Amazing things happen, and we are given the privilege of being the channels of the Holy Spirit's prayer.*

Elisabeth Elliot

# Week 3 - No Fear in Death

## *Day 1 - Saved by Grace*

1.  The fear of death is rooted in the fear of punishment for a lifetime of sin and rebellion against God.  When we are in a right relationship with God, our sins have been forgiven, so we have no reason to fear death.  Jesus took God's wrath against our sins when He died on the Cross in our place.  Jesus bore our death sentence.  Our sins have been replaced with His righteousness.

The fear of death and the fear of eternal punishment are replaced with the love of God and the assurance of eternal life.  Jesus replaced our sin with His righteousness, which put us in a right standing before God, free from sin and condemnation - just as if we had never sinned.

The verses below are known as the *Roman Road* and are often used to witness to unbelievers.  Explain each verse as it applies to your life.

a.  Romans 3:23

b.  Romans 6:23

c. Romans 5:8


d. Romans 10:9


2. Review Romans 5:12-21. Jesus is portrayed as the second Adam as He did what Adam could not do. While Adam gave us sin, condemnation and death, Jesus provides us with righteousness, justification and eternal life. Jesus became one of us to do what we could not do for ourselves. We could never be good enough to stand before a Holy God.

Read Ephesians 2:4-10.

a. How are we saved from God's wrath against sin (v 8-9)?


b. In your own words, explain verse 10.


God is Holy and in order to have a relationship with Him, we must be holy. Our sin and corruption separate us from God. God is merciful and He loves us. Our gracious God created a plan of redemption to make us holy so that we can stand before Him without fear of judgment. His plan is perfect as it allows us to be with Him forever. God's plan gives us hope and a future where we once had neither.

*Death is robbed of much of its terror for the true believer.*

Billy Graham

3. Grief is a painful experience even for believers as demonstrated by Jesus when Lazarus died. While Jesus knew that He would see Lazarus again (very soon), He still grieved. In John 11:33-38, Jesus was deeply moved in His spirit and greatly troubled, and He cried.

a. Jesus loved Lazarus and his sisters, Mary and Martha.

How must Jesus have felt as He saw the pain Mary and Martha were experiencing at the death of their brother?

b. When someone dies that we love, we oftentimes feel anger along with deep sorrow.

Considering the pain of death that started with Adam and Eve and continued throughout all generations, how angry must Jesus have felt at seeing the destruction caused by death to His very special creation - mankind?

4. While death is not punishment for believers, we live in a fallen world and the effects of sin are still a part of it. In our current state, we have not

received the full benefits of salvation as our physical bodies are aging and will eventually die.

Read Romans 8:18-25.

a. Why are the sufferings of this world not comparable to future?

b. What examples do you see in nature that demonstrate a fallen world?

c. What are believers in Christ eagerly waiting and hoping for?

5. When we have *hope* in God, our expectation of fulfillment is with full confidence. God is faithful and unwavering in His promises. In contrast, hope in anything in this life always comes with some degree of doubt or uncertainty.

Read 1 Thessalonians 4:13-18.

a. What hope do we have when fellow believers die?

b. What promise do we have that we will see them again?

c. If you were talking to a grieving Christian about the death of her loved one who died as a believer in Jesus Christ, what would you say to comfort her?

d. Consider the difficulties of this conversation if the deceased was an unbeliever.

Believers do not grieve like the world who has no hope. We grieve knowing the pain of separation is just temporary. Our loved ones cannot come back to us, but we will go to where they are if they died believing in Christ. We will never again feel the terrible pain of loss and separation. Our tears will be replaced with everlasting joy.

*Some day you will read in the papers that D.L. Moody of East Northfield, is dead. Don't you believe a word of it! At that moment I shall be more alive than I am now; I shall have gone up higher, that is all, out of this old clay tenement into a house that is immortal - a body that death cannot touch, that sin cannot taint; a body fashioned like unto His glorious body.*

Dwight L. Moody

6. God's faithfulness in life and death is what gives us eternal assurance.

Read Romans 8:28-30 and 8:34–39.

a. If God has justified us, can we be condemned in death?

b. Who is our intercessor in life and death?

c. How does God reassure us of His love in verses 37-39?

7. The fear of death is a powerful emotion that can easily consume a person and control his or her life. God loves us and He does not want us to live a life of fear and doubt.

a. Read Hebrews 2:14-15.

How does the fear of death cause a life of slavery?

b. Read 1 John 4:15-18.

How is the fear of death conquered?

8. Instead of living a life of bondage in fear of death, God reassures us that those who love Him and practice such love do not need to fear punishment after death. Nothing in this life or the next can separate us from our loving God.

Read Romans 14:8-9.

a. How is Jesus described in these verses?

b. Does our standing with God change when we die?

c. Does this knowledge give you peace instead of fear? Explain.

Fear turns people into self-focused cowards. Satan wants to cripple us with the fear death. He knows that if we are held captive under the bondage of fear, we will do little for the Kingdom of God.

We are to fear God and God alone. To fear the all-powerful God of the universe is the beginning of wisdom.

As His children, we are reassured of God's love. The Father's acceptance of Jesus' work on the Cross gives us confidence to never fear death. Jesus is our Lord whether we are alive or dead. He will never abandon us. As believers, we have an eternal bond with our Lord that cannot be broken. We have no reason to fear death because our God is faithful to His promises.

*Take care of your life and the Lord will take care of your death.*

George Whitefield

## Day 4 - Fearless Testimonies

9. In the face of persecution, we understand that obedience and faithfulness to God are more important than staying physically alive in this temporal body. Eternal life is greater than anything this world has to offer. The Apostle Paul was persecuted to the point of death many times for sharing the Gospel.

Read Acts 21:13 and Philippians 1:19-24.

a. What was Paul willing to do in Jerusalem?

b. How did Paul compare the benefits of his life vs his death?

c. Obedience and faithfulness to the Lord's will was more valuable to Paul than his own life.

How did Paul's attitude toward death compare to yours?

10. Stephen was a devout believer and deacon in the early church (Acts 6:5). He was full of faith and the Holy Spirit. Stephen performed great wonders and signs among the people (Acts 6:8).

Stephen was accused of blasphemy for his faith in Jesus Christ. As a result, he was brought before the religious leaders. In Acts 7:1-53, Stephen responds to his accusers as he explains the Christian faith to the religious council and exposes their hypocrisy and resistance to the Holy Spirit.

Read Acts 7:51-60. This passage includes the ending of Stephen's sermon and the religious leaders' response.

a. How did Stephen's attitude toward death impact his boldness in sharing the Gospel?

b. The religious leaders wanted to permanently silence Jesus and Stephen, so they killed them. While dying, Jesus and Stephen both prayed for their persecutors.

Compare Luke 23:33-34 and Acts 7:60.

How should we feel about those who are seeking to silence or destroy Christians for our faith in Jesus Christ?

c. What vision did Stephen see right before his death (Acts 7:55-56)?

d. How might Stephen have felt when he saw the vision?

e. Stephen was the first martyr of the early church.

What testimony did Stephen leave for all believers?

God's Word is an offense to the world as it reveals their sins. The religious leaders hated Stephen's sermon. The powerful elite hated the Gospel message since it made them irrelevant and wrong in how they had been leading the people. The Gospel message exposed their hypocrisy and pride.

As demonstrated by Stephen, if we love others, we must speak the truth to them in love. Our love for the lost must be greater than our fear of how they might react.

2 Timothy 1:7 states, "For God gave us a spirit not of fear but of power and love and self-control."

If we live in fear of death, we will never be the bold witnesses that God has called us to be. This world does not need Christians who succumb to every cultural shift of ideas, doing so does more harm than good. This world needs to see Christians who are courageous and not ashamed of the Gospel of Jesus Christ.

*Fear of man is the enemy of the fear of the Lord. The fear of man pushes us to perform for man's approval rather than according to God's directives.*

Paul Chappell

11. Jesus willingly suffered and died on the cross for our sins.

Read John 10:17-18.

What did Jesus have the power (or authority) to do?

12. Jesus suffered with pain and anguish at His own death, which enables Him to help us in our sufferings at death.

Read Matthew 16:21.

What did Jesus know beforehand about His own death?

13. When Jesus knew that His death was imminent, He went into the Garden of Gethsemane to pray. In tears of anguish, Jesus prayed - if possible, the bitter cup would pass from Him. Jesus understood God's plan and willingly surrendered even though He knew the fullness of God's wrath against sin would fall on Him.

Read Luke 22:41-44.

How was Jesus' humanity displayed during this time?

14.  Many Old Testament prophecies teach us about the Messiah's (Jesus Christ) birth, life and death.  Isaiah 53 is a prophesy about the promised Messiah.

a.  Read Isaiah 53:3.

How was the Messiah described in verse 3?

b.  Who ultimately put the Messiah to death?  Refer to Isaiah 53:4 and 53:10.  Depending on your Bible translation, look for terms like stricken, smitten, bruised, and punished.

c.  Why did it please God to kill the Messiah?  Consider the ultimate purpose of Jesus' death in your response.

d.  Jesus was holy, pure, and undefiled when our repulsive sins were placed upon Him.  God poured out His full wrath against sin as Jesus hung on the cross.

The pain and anguish Jesus endured is beyond our comprehension.

Read Matthew 27:46.

How did Jesus feel under the crushing weight of humanities' sins and the fullness of God's wrath?

e.  What would you like to say to Jesus for all He endured on the cross on your behalf?

Jesus knew His death would be intensely cruel. Jesus also knew that He had the power and authority to not die. He could have walked away and abandoned the Cross, but doing so would have also meant abandoning us, thereby, eternally damning us all to hell.

By submitting to His Father's will, Jesus proved that His love for us was greater than the horrors of the Cross. No greater love has ever been shown than what Jesus demonstrated to become our Savior.

*Ah, Lord Jesus! I never knew Your love till I understood the meaning of Your death.*

Charles Spurgeon

# Week 4 - Your Last Breath

## Day 1 - Being Made Perfect

1. Death is how God chooses to bring us from this life into the next. God never does us harm as He allows events in our lives to draw us close to Him, including our sufferings and death.

a. Read Hebrews 2:9-11.

Who was made perfect in suffering?

b. Review Hebrews 2:18.

How is Jesus qualified to help us when we are tempted?

c. Read Hebrews 5:7-9.

Prior to His death, Jesus cried and prayed as He was in great turmoil.

What did Jesus learn from His sufferings?

2. Jesus demonstrated obedience to God during His sufferings and death.

a. Read Romans 6:4-11.

How do we share in Jesus' sufferings and death?

b. As we grow in the Lord, we learn to crucify the sinful flesh as we are led by the Holy Spirit to obey God's Word.

Read Romans 8:14-17.

How do we share in His resurrection?

3. Our faithfulness to God is more important than our sufferings and death.

a. Read 2 Corinthians 4:16 18.

How do the sufferings of this life compare to eternal glory?

b. Read 1 Peter 5:8-10.

What happens after we have suffered for a while?

c. Read Hebrews 12:1-3.

How do we run the race with endurance?

With every trial, we learn faith and obedience as God draws us close to Himself. Our sufferings and death are how God chooses to transform us into His image bearers as His sons and daughters. One day we will understand His workings in our lives and thank Him for everything He did to help us learn to trust Him.

*The best we can hope for in this life is a knothole peek at the shining realities ahead. Yet a glimpse is enough. It's enough to convince our hearts that whatever sufferings and sorrows currently assail us aren't worthy of comparison to that which waits over the horizon.*

Joni Eareckson Tada

## *Day 2 - Jesus is Our Escort*

4. As Jesus was dying on the cross, when His work was complete, Jesus said, "It is finished" (John 19:30) and "Father, into Your hands I commit My spirit" (Luke 23:46). Jesus demonstrated unwavering devotion and trust to His Father in life and death.

Not only did Jesus teach us how to live, but He taught us how to die. He demonstrated on the cross with His last words that we too can trust God with our very souls. We will not be forgotten by God.

Read Luke 12:4-7.

How does this passage give you assurance when thinking about your own death?

5. Consider the following passages that we've read in prior lessons:

a. Review Romans 8:38-39.

As we've learned, God's love is eternal and absolutely nothing can stop Him from loving you. Not even death can separate us from God's love.

Does this realization give you confidence that God will not forsake you in death?

b. Review Psalm 139:7-8.

God is everywhere, all the time. No matter where we go, even after death, God is there.

Does knowing that God is going to be with you calm your concerns about the unknown aspects of death?

c. Review Acts 7:55-56.

When Stephen was being stoned to death, Jesus stood up. Jesus was standing and watching, ready to receive Stephen when he died.

Does knowing that Jesus will be watching over your death, as He stands ready to receive you, give you peace?

6. God's Word is teaching us not to be fearful or anxious about death. He is always near. We can have comfort in knowing that our Lord is our escort as we pass from this life into the next.

Read Psalm 23 and summarize this passage in your own words.

Jesus carries us over the threshold of death like a groom carries his new bride over the threshold as they enter the home that he has prepared for her. Satan wants us to dread our death, but Jesus is eagerly awaiting the arrival of His bride.

*Take care of your life and the Lord will take care of your death.*

George Whitefield

## Day 3 - The Sleep of Death

7. In both the Old and New Testament, the dead were also referred to as being asleep. The dead body is lifeless and unable to communicate with those who are still alive on earth. The dead body in the grave is a temporary condition just like sleep is temporary.

a. Read Psalm 13:3.

How is death described by David?

b. Read Ecclesiastes 9:4-6.

How does Solomon describe a dead person's ability to share in life on this earth?

8. Review John 11:11-15.

How did Jesus initially describe Lazarus's condition?

What did Jesus make plain to the disciples?

9. When Stephen was martyred, how was his death described in Acts 7:60.




10. Read 1 Thessalonians 4:14.

Finish this verse, "For since we believe that Jesus died and rose again, even

so, through Jesus, God will bring with Him _____


_____."




11. Read 1 Corinthians 15:12-23.

Note: First fruits means the first portion or the firstlings, such as the first fruits harvested or the first animal offspring of a season.

a. How is Christ the first fruits of believers who have died?



b. In verse 19, why should we be pitied if everything we had hoped for as believers in Christ is only received in this life?

c. How does the reality of Christ's resurrection give us assurance?

Our hope and assurance is beyond this life.  We will live again because our Savior rose from the grave and He lives.  Just like sleep, death is temporary.  All people will be raised from the grave.  Believers will be raised to everlasting life and unbelievers to eternal damnation.

*We'll say good night here and good morning up there.*

John R. Rice

# Day 4 - The Body and Soul Separate

12. God's spirit sustains all life. Every living thing depends daily on God's Spirit to keep it alive. Every heartbeat is a heartbeat from God. According to the following Scriptures, what happens to your body and spirit (or soul) when you die?

a. Psalm 104:29

b. Psalm 146:4

c. Ecclesiastes 12:7

13. When God removes His life-sustaining Spirit, the heart stops beating and the body and soul (or spirit) separate. The lifeless, physical body stays on earth, starts decaying, and eventually returns to dust. Our soul returns to God for His safe keeping as we await our resurrection.

Read Job 34:14-15.

What would happen to all humanity if God took away His spirit and His breath?



14. Read Colossians 1:17 and finish the sentence, "He is before all things, and in Him

_____."



15. At death, your soul (or spirit) goes to one of two places. When believers die their souls go home to be with the Lord. When unbelievers die, God maintains their souls while they await final judgment. This teaching is consistent in both the Old and New Testament.

*Sheol* is a general term for the grave in the Old Testament for both believers and unbelievers. Sheol is a Hebrew word meaning grave or abode of the dead. In the New Testament, the Greek word *Hades* is used as the equivalent to *Sheol*.

Paradise and Abraham's Bosom are also mentioned as a place of comfort where believers go after death. Hell, or Gehenna is described as a place of torment reserved for unbelievers.

What do the following Old and New Testament verses teach about the grave?

a. Psalm 9:17 - Where do the wicked go?




b. Psalm 6:5 - Can the dead publicly praise God?




c. 1 Samuel 2:6 - Who is in control of Sheol?




d. Mark 9:43 - How did Jesus describe hell?




e. Matthew 10:28 - What warning did Jesus give?

Life is from God.  Without Him, nothing exist.  When we die, our bodies return to dust and our souls return to God for His safe keeping until we are resurrected from the dead.  God is the keeper of all dead souls, believers and unbelievers.  While believers and unbelievers go to different places, God is still in control of where we are and what we are able to do and feel.

*What a compelling motive we have for prayer, for preaching, for soul winning when we learn that every responsible human being who leaves this world without a definite change in heart immediately lifts his eyes in Hell, tormented in flame!*

John R. Rice

16. Cremation vs burial is a very personal decision that challenges many grieving hearts. Some people believe that it is dishonorable or disrespectful to cremate someone. Others simply cannot afford the cost of a funeral; therefore, cremation is their only option.

While the Bible does not provide a clear directive on acceptable and unacceptable burial practices, we can look at examples in Scripture to help us make informed decisions.

The traditional Hebrew practice in both the Old and New Testament was to bury the dead. Abraham purchased a burial place for Sarah. Later, Abraham and his children were also buried near Sarah (Genesis 23 and 49:31).

Joseph was buried in Egypt and, in accordance with his dying request, his bones were taken when the children of Israel went into the promised land (Genesis 50:24-26 and Joshua 24:32). Stephen and Lazarus were both buried (Acts 8:2 and John 11).

Read John 19:40. Jesus' burial was done in keeping with

_____.

17. The Bible also provides examples of dead bodies being burned (cremated). When Achan was convicted of a terrible sin, he was stoned to death and his body was burned (Joshua 7:15, 25).

Faithful people were also burned, including Jonathan, King Saul's son.

a. Read 1 Samuel 31:11-13.

How was the body of Saul and his sons (including Jonathan) disposed of?

b. David loved Jonathan and respected Saul as king. After Saul and his sons' bodies were burned, their remaining bones were buried.

Read 2 Samuel 2:4-6.

Did David determine this was an acceptable way to dispose of their remains?

18. While Paul was teaching on the importance of love, he referenced the burning of martyrs.

Read 1 Corinthians 13:3.

Did Paul honor or dishonor believers who were burned?

19.  Many people die without the opportunity for a burial of their full body. Throughout history people have been burned, beheaded, eaten by animals, dismembered on the battlefield or ripped apart in tragic accidents.  Many people with good intentions have given their bodies to science, and a number of people have had diseased organs or limbs removed to save their lives.  Others have received organ transplants from living and dead donors. Even so, God is able to resurrect their dead corpse.

As we have already learned, when we die our bodies return to dust, so it can be argued that cremation just speeds up the process.  God does not lose track of us at death, regardless of whether our bodies are fully intact or broken into tiny dust molecules scattered all over the land and sea.

When we are resurrected from the dead, we will be given a new, imperishable body.  These old, decaying bodies are not our eternal structure.  Since we will be given a new body, there is no need to get overly attached to the current one.

Read 1 Corinthians 15:42-44.


How will our resurrected bodies differ from our current fleshly bodies?


*When people die, only their bodies go into the grave. At the funeral it is merely the physical shell we see lying in the casket. The real person, the soul/spirit, has already departed to either a place of torment or a place of comfort, depending on the person's spiritual condition.*

Charles Swindoll

# Week 5 - The Soul Continues to Exist

1. Old Testament believers had full confidence that they would be with God after they died.

How do the following passages reflect the writers' confidence that they would be in the presence of God after their deaths?

a. Psalm 23:6

b. Job 19:25-27

2. Jesus confirmed that Old Testament believers are still *"alive"* when He disputed the Sadducees who claimed there was no resurrection of the dead.

Read Matthew 22:31-32.

Finish this sentence, "He is not God of the dead,

_____."

3.  This message is continued in the New Testament as dead believers are said to be at home with the Lord.

How do the following passages indicate believers go immediately into the presence of God at death?

a.  Luke 23:42-43

b.  2 Corinthians 5:6-8

c.  Philippians 1:21-24

4.  Believers go home to be *with the Lord* immediately upon death.  When Jesus was resurrected from the grave, He ascended into the clouds.

a.  Read Ephesians 1:20.

Where did Jesus go after completing His work on the cross?

b.  Review Acts 7:55-56.

Right before Stephen died, he looked up to heaven being filled with the Holy Spirit and saw the glory of God.

Where was Jesus when Stephen saw Him?

c.  Based on the Scriptures above, where will believers go immediately after death if to be absent from the body is to be present with the Lord?

5.  With every breath we draw closer to our last as our Heavenly Father eagerly awaits our arrival to welcome us home.

a.  Read Psalm 116:15.

Why is our death precious to God?

b. The prophet Isaiah longed to be with God as he writes in Isaiah 26:9, "My soul yearns for You in the night; my spirit within me earnestly seeks You."

Reflect on how you are responding to God's love.

Do you yearn to be with Him?

Jesus is now seated in the heavenly places at the right hand of God the Father. Scripture reassures us that if we die as believers in Christ, we immediately go into the presence of the Lord. We will be with our Lord in Paradise - a heavenly place of comfort, joy and rest. Never again will we feel the pains and sorrows of this life. Our hell on earth will be over!

*I have a certainty about eternity that is a wonderful thing, and I thank God for giving me that certainty. I do not fear death. I may fear a little bit about the process, but not death itself, because I think the moment that my spirit leaves this body, I will be in the presence of the Lord.*

Billy Graham

6. Jesus provided insight into what happens when unbelievers die in the story about Lazarus and the rich man. While some Bible scholars think this is a parable, many do not. This story is unique compared to other parables since one of the characters - Lazarus, was specifically named; and Jesus did not explain this story whereas He did explain other parables. Regardless of whether this story is a real event or a parable, Jesus had a purpose for telling it.

Read Luke 16:19-31 and consider Jesus 'main teaching points as He contrasts the deaths of two men: one was righteous and the other was wicked.

a. The rich man lived in overabundance and gluttony as he passed by the poor, hungry and sick man named Lazarus at his gate every day.

Did the rich man offer to help Lazarus?

b. Where did Lazarus's soul go after he died?

c.  This story does not condemn all rich people.  Instead, it illustrates the importance of not living selfish lives with no concern for others.

Where did the (wicked) rich man's soul go after he died?

d.  How did Lazarus feel after his death?

Was he in comfort?

Were his earthly pains and sorrows gone?

e.  How did the rich man feel after his death?

Was he in comfort or torment?

Were his earthly pleasures and comforts gone?

f.  After his death, could the rich man repent and go to be with Lazarus?

If no, why not?

Jesus' story also teaches against the view of the total annihilation of unbelievers. Immediately after death, we all wake up in eternity somewhere. The wicked man's soul continued. He was conscious and in torment. He also could not change his status. He was not able to cross from his place of torment into Lazarus's place of comfort. The wicked rich man lived a selfish life, focusing on his own pleasures while ignoring the needs of others. He failed to cherish his soul. He did not take God or eternity seriously.

Unbelievers have a harsh reality when they die. They immediately leave all the good they will ever experience and are immediately transported to a place of unbearable separation from their loving Creator. Never again will they feel the cool of the day or hear a child laugh. Feelings of peace, joy, and hope are forever gone and replaced with pain, isolation and hopelessness.

*Don't say that a loving God is going to send you to hell - He's not. The thing that's going to send you to hell is that you're a sinner and you don't want to admit it.*

J. Vernon McGee

8. The Bible does not teach the doctrine of "soul sleep" or unconscious existence in death. Instead, we read about souls who are alert and communicating.

Our ability to communicate on earth ends at our death. Dead people are unable to speak or praise God in this life - on this earth. However, the believer's ability to praise God never ceases; it does not end at our death.

Read Psalm 115:17-18.

a. When do believers bless the Lord?

b. Does our ability to praise God ever end?

9. As discussed in the prior lesson, Jesus taught about the soul when He contrasted the death of a wicked rich man and a poor man named Lazarus. This story is told in Luke 16:19-31. The rich man's soul was in Hades and Lazarus's soul was with Abraham in Paradise (Abraham's Bosom). Abraham was able to communicate in Paradise, and the rich man was able to communicate in Hades, which indicates their souls were conscious and

engaged. While in Hades, the rich man was in torment which shows his ability to feel pain.

Consider the following observations that further demonstrate the soul's abilities after death.

a. Could the rich man see Abraham and Lazarus?

b. Was the rich man able to have a conversation with Abraham?

c. Was Abraham able to hear the rich man and respond?

d. Did the rich man retain his memory of people he knew on earth?

10. Scripture provides examples of souls communicating prior to being reunited with their resurrected bodies.

Read Revelation 6:9-11.

a. Who was under the altar?

b. What are they doing?

c. Are they able to speak?

d. What are they wearing?

e. What do they want?

11. As we've learned in Philippians 1:23 and 2 Corinthians 5:8, death is far better for believers because when our soul leaves the body, we go home to be with the Lord - a place of safety, joy and contentment. These passages imply a conscious state that is better than this earthly life.

a. While hanging on the cross, how did Jesus respond to the believing thief's request, "Remember me when You come in Your kingdom"? Refer to Luke 23:43.

b. The thief died on the same day as Jesus. His body and soul separated.

How long did the thief need to wait to be with the Lord?

c. Do you think Jesus would have said these words to the dying thief if his soul was going to be in a state of unconsciousness?

d. Do you find comfort in Jesus' words?  Explain.

Believers have something to look forward to in death.  We will be with Jesus in paradise as soon as we breath our last breath.  We will be engaged with our Lord and able to praise Him.  Somehow, we will be able to see and communicate.  We will be with other believers as together we wait with our Lord until the time of His second coming.

*Every life is precious to God.  God created every one of us. He gave us a soul, and that soul will live as long as God lives.*

Franklin Graham

## Day 4 - Communicating with the Dead

12. When our loved ones die, we miss them terribly and would give anything to engage in just one more conversation. For this reason, many people will go to a grave site and talk to the ground in which their loved ones are buried. Others will seek mediums or spiritual guides in efforts to communicate with the dead. The term medium, diviner, familiar spirit, spiritist, spiritualist, or necromancer are used in Scripture to describe people who practice witchcraft, sorcery, occultism, and magic. Today, we also refer to them as fortune tellers, palm readers, tea leaf readers, and so on.

a. Read Leviticus 19:31.

Why are we warned to stay away from mediums or spiritists (necromancers)?

b. Read Leviticus 20:27.

What was the punishment under the Law for being a medium or spiritist?

c. Read Deuteronomy 18:10-14.

Why does God prohibit us from trying to communicate with the dead?

13.  In 1 Samuel 28, we learn about a time when the deceased prophet Samuel was consulted.  The Philistine army was threatening Israel, and King Saul was terrified.  Saul inquired of the Lord with no response, so he consulted a medium at Endor in efforts to communicate with Samuel.  In 1 Samuel 28:11-19, when the deceased prophet appears, the medium screams as she is stunned that Samuel actually appeared.  Mediums' normal tricks include deception and using evil spirits to provide familiar information or impersonate dead people.

Samuel's appearance is the only occurrence of communication with the dead recorded in Scripture and this detestable act did not go well for Saul.  Samuel rebukes Saul for calling him up from the grave and prophesies that Saul and his sons would be killed the next day.

Read 1 Chronicles 10:13-14.

Why did Saul die?

Note:  Some question whether the spirit was the deceased Samuel or just an evil spirit impersonating the prophet.  The fact that the spirit predicted the future supports the understanding that this was Samuel speaking from the grave. Only true prophets of God can predict the future with perfect accuracy.

14. To seek the assistance of a spiritualist demonstrates a lack of faith in God and a naive yielding to demonic spirits.

Read the following warnings from the New Testament. What do you learn about deceiving spirits?

a. 1 Timothy 4:1-2

b. 1 Corinthians 10:20-21

c. 2 Corinthians 11:13-14

d. 2 Thessalonians 2:8-12

*Many deceptions only appeal to us because there is something inside us that "wants" to believe them. They are seductive because of darkness and wrong motives in our own lives. We must search our hearts and root these out.*

Andrew Strom

15. The doctrine of purgatory is not taught in the Bible. Many religions teach some form of purgatory as a temporary state where the souls of believers go to be purified from their sins before entering heaven. They suffer in purgatory as punishments for sins that were not punished while on earth.

Based on what Jesus taught about Lazarus and the rich man in Luke 16:19-31, was the rich man able to pay penance and leave his place of torment?

16. Supporters of the doctrine of purgatory use Matthew 12:31-32 and 1 Corinthians 3:15 to support their position.

How do you interpret these verses?

Consider the following.

Those who believe in purgatory see Matthew 12:31-32 as a possibility that sins can be forgiven later in the "age to come." This passage does not open the door for a later forgiveness of sins. Instead, it speaks to the unique situation of blasphemy against the Holy Spirit for which Jesus was warning the Pharisees against.

1 Corinthians 3:15 discusses that our works on earth will be judged and tested by fire. We will not receive rewards for works that are burned up. This verse does not say that a person will be burned or punished in the fire. Instead, our works will be tested to reveal good works that are worthy of an eternal reward. We will discuss eternal rewards in a later lesson.

17. Another problem with the doctrine of purgatory is that it requires works or a payment in the form of punishments in order to gain entrance into heaven.

Read Ephesians 2:8-9.

Can we work our way into heaven?

18. Read Hebrews 9:27.

How does this verse also refute the doctrine of purgatory?

Those who believe in purgatory also spend countless hours praying for the dead. As we've already learned, at death the souls of believers immediately go into the presence of God. Therefore, we no longer need to pray for dead believers or worry about them.

Unbelievers go immediately into a place of torment and separation from God. Their eternal status cannot be changed. Repentance is no longer an option. Therefore, to pray for dead unbelievers is futile.

The eternal fate of believers and unbelievers is finalized at their death. To continue to pray for them in efforts to change their eternal destiny is a false hope. Instead, turn your attention to the living.

*God keeps no half-way house. It's either heaven or hell for you and me.*

Billy Sunday

# Week 6 - The Second Coming of Christ

Since the focus of this Bible study is death and the hereafter, time does not permit sufficient debate on the differing views of eschatology including the rapture, antichrist, tribulation and millennium period. Instead, we will turn our attention to Jesus' second coming and its impact on mankind for all eternity.

## Day 1 - This Same Jesus Will Return

1. After Jesus's death, burial and resurrection, He appeared before His followers several times. Jesus' last appearance was immediately before His ascension into heaven. Before departing earth, Jesus gave His followers the Great Commission: through the power of the Holy Spirit, they are to be His witnesses throughout the world.

Read Acts 1:9-11.

What assurance did the two men dressed in white clothing tell the onlookers?

2. Jesus will return in a personal, bodily form. Jesus was fully God and fully human when He left and He will return in like manner. He did not change after He ascended into heaven. His ascension was visible. His return will likewise be visible.

How do the following passages describe Jesus' return?

a. 1 Thessalonians 4:16

b. Revelation 1:7

3. Everything God does is for a purpose. What do the following verses state as the purpose for Jesus' return to earth?

a. John 14:3

b. Hebrews 9:28

c. Revelation 22:12-13

The same Jesus who ascended into heaven is the exact same Jesus who will return. He's coming back for those who love Him and are called by His name. Jesus is the author of the history of mankind. His plans were set in motion before the world was created, and His plans will continue to unfold exactly how He predetermined until all is finished. He's the Alpha and Omega - the beginning and the end, and He's our soon coming King!

*Preach [and live] as if Jesus was crucified yesterday, rose from the dead today, and is returning tomorrow.*

Martin Luther

4. Believers have been debating the date of Jesus' second coming since the day He ascended into heaven. While no one knows for sure when Christ will return, we can all agree that with each passing day, His return draws closer.

a. Read Matthew 24:44 and Luke 12:40.

When did Jesus say He would return?

b. Read Mark 13:32-33.

Who knows when Jesus will return?

5. Jesus will return to the same location from which He ascended.

a. Read Acts 1:11-12.

Where was Jesus when He ascended into heaven?

b. Read Zechariah 14:3-4.

Where will the Lord return?

6. No one knows the exact date that Jesus will return. We only know that He will return at a time no one expects. He ascended from the Mount of Olives and He will return to the Mount of Olives. The Mount of Olives is on the east side of Jerusalem's Old City.

What do the following passages tell us to do as we await the return of our Lord and Savior, Jesus Christ?

a. Matthew 25:13

b. Titus 2:11-13

c. Revelation 22:10-12

As believers, we are to be on alert as we eagerly await our Lord's return.

Guard against Satan's lies of deception and worldly lusts. Deny ungodliness and practice righteousness as we share the Good News of Jesus Christ and serve as His witnesses to the world. Do good works while we still have time.

*Do Christians in fact eagerly long for Christ's return? The more Christians are caught up in enjoying the good things of this life, and the more they neglect genuine Christian fellowship and their personal relationship with Christ, the less they will long for his return.*

Wayne Grudem

## Day 3 - Resurrection of Believers

7. When Jesus returns, our bodies will be resurrected and our bodies and souls will reunite. The reunited body and soul will be transformed into our eternal bodies.

a. Read John 11:25-26.

Who will be resurrected into eternal life?

b. Read 1 Corinthians 6:14.

By whose power will we be raised from the dead?

c. Read 1 Thessalonians 4:16-17.

When will believers be resurrected and who among them will be resurrected first?

8. After Jesus was resurrected, He appeared to His disciples, but they thought He was a spirit.

Read Luke 24:36-43.

How did Jesus demonstrate that He was still human in His resurrected body?

9.  Read 1 John 3:2 and Philippians 3:20-21.

How will our resurrected bodies compare to Jesus' resurrected body?

10.  Like Jesus, our new bodies will be physical.  We will live in bodily form and be able to eat, drink, walk, and talk.

Read 1 Corinthians 15:42-49.

a.  How will our new heavenly bodies be different from our earthly bodies?

Note:  As you read this passage, the "natural" body is referring to carnal flesh.  The "spiritual" body is non-carnal, filled with and governed by the Holy Spirit.

b.  How does the earthly body compare to the resurrected body?

List as many details you can find.

Earthly Body                              Resurrected Body

When Jesus returns, all believers - living and dead, will be raised to meet Him.  Our bodies and souls will be reunited as we are given incorruptible bodies that bear the image of God.  Like Jesus, our new glorified bodies will be both physical and spiritual.  Our new bodies will last for all eternity with no possibility of decay.  We will never age, get sick, or feel pain. Everything that was a thorn in our earthly flesh will be forever gone.  We will still be the same person; except we will be perfect.

*He alone can believe in immortality who feels the resurrection in him already.*
Frederick W. Robertson

11. The first man and woman were created in the image of God. As a result of sin, humanity now bears a distorted image of God, but not forever. When Jesus returns, He will make all things new and restore what was lost in the Fall including the human race as God's true and complete image bearers.

We will be incorruptible, both physically and spiritually. We will no longer have the desire or ability to sin. We will never get sick or grow old. Our bodies will be perfect, strong and vigorous. Our minds will be sharp and working at full capacity. We will be what God originally intended in the Garden of Eden.

When Jesus raised Lazarus from the dead, He told Martha (Lazarus's sister), "Did I not say to you that if you believe you will see the glory of God?" (John 11:40). Likewise, our resurrection will manifest the glory of God as it demonstrates something that only God can accomplish.

Read Romans 8:28-30.

*Glorified* is defined as to clothe with splendor, to make glorious, to hold with honor, to cause the dignity and worth of someone to become manifest and acknowledged.

a. Who will be glorified by God?

b. How does this passage illustrate God's work in the lives and resurrection of those who love Him?

12. We will be transformed from dishonorable to glorious.

a. Peter, James and John got a glimpse of Jesus' glorified body at the Transfiguration.

Read Matthew 17:2.

How did Jesus look in His transfigured, glorious body?

b. God appeared to Moses in a cloud on Mount Sinai.

Read Exodus 34:29-30.

How did Moses look after being in the presence of God?

c. Read Daniel 12:3 and Matthew 13:43.

How do the following verses describe the glory of the saints?


How long will their glory shine?



Note: A few illustrations in Scripture make Bible students wonder if our new, eternal bodies will be able to defy the rules of nature such as gravity and space. After Jesus was raised from the dead, He appeared in His resurrected body to His disciples twice while they were in a room with a locked door (John 20:19, 26). Before His death, Jesus also demonstrated that He could walk on water (Matthew 14:25-27) and pass through the midst of an angry crowd without them seeing Him (Luke 4:30).

After baptizing the Ethiopian eunuch on the road from Jerusalem to Gaza, Phillip was miraculously transported by the Spirit to Azotus (Acts 8:39-40). Scripture does not provide sufficient detail to know the full extent of our heavenly capabilities, but they will be glorious and we will be like Him.

*Jesus Christ did not come into this world to make bad people good; He came into this world to make dead people live.*

Lee Strobel

## Day 5 - Judgment of Believers' Works

13.  While judgment day is coming for all of us, all of us will not be at the same judgment.  Believers will be judged separately than unbelievers and for different reasons.

Read John 5:24-29.

a.  What are the two types of resurrections and who participates in each?

b.  Do believers come under judgment?

14.  In Paul's letter to the church of God at Corinth, he refers to the judgment of believers.  The term "judgment seat" for believers is also known as the Bema Seat.

a.  Read 2 Corinthians 5:10.

Describe why believers will appear before the judgment seat of Christ.

b.  Read 1 Corinthians 3:12-15.

Our works will be revealed to determine if they are valuable or worthless. Works done in pride or with selfish motives, for example, will burn up. True works glorify God and not us.

If a believer's works are entirely burned up, will he still be saved?

15. As believers, our sins have been forgiven. Romans 8:1 reassures us, "There is therefore now no condemnation for those who are in Christ Jesus." This passage refutes any future punishment or purgatory for believers. Rewards are based on good works; salvation is based on God's grace.

Consider the definition of rewards. Rewards are the consequence of good behavior and are used as motivation for the achiever. Our appearance before the Bema Seat is purely to receive our rewards for our good works done in this life. The rewards of believers are often referred to as crowns and serve as motivators to faithfulness.

a. Read 1 Corinthians 9:25.

How is the believer's crown (or wreath) different from wreaths won by athletes?

b. Read 1 Thessalonians 2:19-20 and Philippians 4:1.

How does Paul describe his beloved brethren?


c. Read 2 Timothy 4:7-8.

Who will receive the crown of righteousness?


d. Read 1 Peter 5:2-4.

Who will receive the crown of glory?


e. Read James 1:12.

Who will receive the crown of life?


16. The purpose of the crowns is illustrated in Revelations 4:10-11.

a. What do the 24 elders do with their crowns?

b.  To whom do our crowns ultimately bring glory?

Believers will not come under judgment for sin.  God nailed our transgressions to the Cross - our sin debt has been cancelled (Colossians 2:13-14).  Instead of receiving punishment, we will receive rewards. Believers will stand before the judgment (Bema) seat of Christ and be rewarded for our good works.

Believers' rewards are described as crowns and serve to keep us focused on the finish line as we run this race of endurance.  While the idea of future rewards motivates us to faithfulness, the ultimate purpose of our rewards will be to bring God glory as we cast our crowns at His feet.

*At the end of your life on earth you will be evaluated and rewarded according to how well you handled what God entrusted to you.*

Rick Warren

# Week 7 - Righteous Judgment

## Day 1 - Jesus Warns of Coming Judgment

1. In Jesus' sermon on the Mount of Olives, also known as the Olivet Discourse, He taught about coming judgments.

Read Matthew 25:31-46.

a. What judgment do the sheep receive and why?

b. What judgment do the goats receive and why?

c. How long do the judgments last?

2. Judas Iscariot famously betrayed Jesus with a kiss. On judgment day we will see that Judas was not the only one to betray the Lord. Jesus warns of hypocrisy as many will claim to know Him but they do not.

Read Matthew 7:13-29.

a.  Where does the wide gate lead, and how many enter through it?

b.  What happens to the tree that does not bear good fruit?

c.  Who will Jesus deny knowing and why?

d.  Describe the differences between the wise man and the foolish man.

e.  Why was the crowd amazed at Jesus' teaching?

Scripture oftentimes refers to believers as sheep and unbelievers as goats. Every person is considered either a sheep or a goat and will be judged accordingly. No one fools God. He sees our hearts and rightly judges our motives and actions. Jesus knows the ones who genuinely believe in Him and those who do not.

Some modern views of heaven and hell are in stark contrast to Jesus' teachings on this subject. They believe the majority of people will go to heaven as they declare, "A good God wouldn't send someone to hell." Jesus, on the other hand, paints a much different picture. He is righteous and just. His warnings of coming judgments should be taken seriously. Jesus is the authority on this subject; others are not.

*I believe that a great number of people are going to die and go to hell because they're counting on their religiosity in the church instead of their relationship with Jesus to get them to heaven. They give lip service to repentance and faith, but they've never been born again.*

Adrian Rogers

3.  The first time Jesus came to earth; His mission was not to judge the world but that the world through Him might be saved.

Read John 3:16 and 3:36.

Who will receive God's wrath instead of eternal life?

4.  When Jesus returns, He will not come to die again for our sins.

Read Revelation 22:12.

What will Jesus do when He returns?

5.  In order for judgments to be enforceable, fair and equitable, the judge must have authority and his rulings must be unbiased and just.

a.  Read John 5:22.

From whom does Jesus get His authority as the judge of humanity?

b. Read Revelation 19:11.

How is the judge described?

c. Read 2 Timothy 4:8 and John 5:30.

How do we know His judgments are fair?

6. As we've already learned, believers will be resurrected at Jesus' second coming. Believers will not face condemnation since our sins have been forgiven. Instead, we will be judged and rewarded for our good works that we accomplished while on earth. Believers' resurrection is referred to as the first resurrection, and we will not participate in the final judgment nor the second death. We are assured, "Blessed and holy is the one who shares in the first resurrection! Over such the second death has no power" (Revelation 20:6).

In contrast, unbelievers will be raised from the dead in order to stand before Jesus and be judged for their sins while on earth.

Read Romans 14:12 and Hebrews 9:27.

Does anyone escape judgment day?

7.  Following Jesus' second coming, Scripture teaches of a millennium period that will occur before the final judgments.  Since an in-depth study of eschatology is beyond the scope of this Bible study, we will turn our focus to the events that follow the millennium period.

Read Revelation 19:20 and 20:10.

a.  List the three who are thrown into the lake of fire.

b.  For how long will they be tormented?

Read Revelation 20:11-15.

c.  What is the judgment seat called?

d.  Who stands before the throne?

e.  What illustration is used in this passage to help us understand that God has recorded all things throughout all of history (v. 12)?

f.  Where do all the dead who are being judged come from?

g.  On what basis are they being judged?

h.  What is their judgment?

i.  Who is already there (refer to your responses to questions a and b above)?

Jesus came the first time into the world to fulfill His role as the Savior. When He returns, He will fulfill His role as the Judge. He is Faithful and True as He comes riding in on a white horse to righteously judge the world. He sits down on His great white throne and opens the books of recorded history. Only those whose names are not written in the book of life will stand before the great white throne. The unbelieving dead will be raised and judged for their deeds while on earth. Since they did not believe in

Jesus while they were alive, their sins are not forgiven.  Therefore, God's wrath will be upon them.  They will be thrown into the eternal lake of fire along with Satan, the fallen angels, the antichrist and the false prophet.


*All roads lead to the judgment seat of Christ.*

Keith Green

8. In order for a judgment to be equitable, the judge needs to know all the relevant facts and circumstances. How do the following verses indicate that Jesus knows everything He needs to know in order to judge without error?

a. Jeremiah 16:17

b. Ecclesiastes 12:14

c. Luke 12:2

d. Romans 2:16

9. God's judgments will be all-inclusive. Every nation will be judged and every unbelieving person will be condemned for their rejection of Jesus Christ. As we learned in the prior lesson, both the small and the great will stand before the great white throne of judgment.

Do the famous, powerful or wealthy have an advantage in death?

10. Revelation 20:12 explains that the books were opened and another book was opened, the book of life. Anyone whose name is not written in the book of life is thrown into the lake of fire. The book of life is also referred to as the Lamb's book of life and the heavenly book. Both the Old and New Testaments reference this book.

a. Read Daniel 12:1.

Who is rescued from the time of distress?

b. Read Luke 10:20.

Why should we rejoice?

c. Read Revelation 3:5.

What three things are promised to those who overcome?

d. Read Revelation 13:7-8. This passage is referring to the antichrist's rule on earth during the Tribulation period.

Who will not worship the antichrist?

e. Read Revelation 21:27. This passage is referring to the future home of believers in Christ, referred to as New Jerusalem.

Who will not be granted entrance into New Jerusalem?

Scripture teaches that the names were written in the book of life before the world was created. God's predetermined plans and foreknowledge work in unison as believers are made perfect in Christ.

Note: Theologians debate the other books mentioned in Revelation 20:12. Regardless of their titles, the books referenced at the great white throne of judgment are opened for a purpose. They represent factual and historical evidence of the actions and motives of those being judged. All is revealed; nothing is hidden. For example, the book of remembrance is alluded to in Malachi 3:16.

*For this time, it will be God without disguise; something so overwhelming that it will strike either irresistible love or irresistible horror into every creature.  It will be too late then to choose your side.*

C.S. Lewis

11. Many of today's churches have succumbed to the pressures of our modern culture and have sadly watered-down the gospel to make their message more appealing to the masses. As a result, they teach that all or at least most people will eventually be saved. Only the devil, fallen angels, the antichrist, the false prophet plus a few murderous dictators like Mao Zedong, Joseph Stalin and Adolf Hitler will end up in hell or the lake of fire.

Another common false teaching is the idea of total annihilation, which is the complete destruction of unbelievers. Instead of being tormented in hell for all eternity, they simply cease to exist perhaps after an appropriate time of punishment.

While the idea of hell being empty and heaven being full sounds wonderful, especially to those of us who have unsaved loved ones, God's Word cannot be twisted to say something more palatable. This is God's universe and what He says goes. Any effort to dilute Scripture is an effort in futility. We cannot reason away what God has predetermined and foretold. Jesus Christ has already determined the extent of hell. As we previously learned in Matthew 7 and 25, the gate is wide and many will enter into it.

Read Matthew 13:40-42, 49-50.

How does Jesus describe the torment of those thrown into the fire?

12. Read Mark 9:42-48.

Jesus is teaching on the importance of self-examination in order to remove sins from our lives. He is quoting from Isaiah in which the dead corpses of wicked men are being eaten by worms as their bodies burn. Both the worms and fire do not cease.

Read Isaiah 66:24.

How will the rest of mankind feel about those who are burning?

13. The purpose of unbelievers' judgment is not to reveal anything to God. God knows everything, including the condition of each person's heart. He knows every thought and every deed - both good and bad. This courtroom will show every person that God is fair and just as each individual is held accountable for his or her sins and rebellion against Him. They are without excuse (Romans 1:19-21).

While all unbelievers are worthy of eternal damnation, some have committed more horrific sins with greater magnitude against humanity and

God. Therefore, many scholars believe that there will be varying degrees of punishment in hell, which further explains the need for individual judgment before sentencing.

How do the following verses provide insight into the idea of degrees of punishment?

a. Revelation 22:12

b. Matthew 16:27

c. Luke 12:47-48

d. Hebrews 10:29

Today, many reject the biblical teachings on hell. Considering that Jesus taught about hell often as He described it as a place of everlasting torment, hell is something to be taken seriously. God's wrath will be against those who transgress against Him. God's judgments will be equitable and His punishments will be appropriate. If we love the world, we must warn them of coming judgment. To do anything less demonstrates a lack of love.

*What fools are they who, for a drop of pleasure, drink a sea of wrath.*

Thomas Watson

## Day 5 - Death is Destroyed

14. Death is our enemy and it will be the last enemy destroyed when Jesus returns. Death entered the world as a result of the Fall - Adam and Eve's sin. Jesus proved that He has power over death when He was resurrected from the dead on the third day.

Read Revelation 1:17-18.

John sees Jesus in his vision.

What illustration does Jesus use to denote His authority over death?

15. Review Revelation 20:13-15.

Jesus uses His authority over death and Hades to call up the unbelieving dead for judgment. After receiving their judgment, unbelievers are thrown into the lake of fire where they are eternally separated from God.

When unbelievers are thrown into the lake of fire, their sins go with them (since their sins have not been forgiven). Death and Hades will also be thrown into the lake of fire. This is known as the second death.

Sin and death will be totally annihilated from heaven and earth. Sin and death are co-dependent; they need each other to exist. Where there is no sin, there is no death. Sin will end; therefore, death will end.

As we already learned, believers will be given incorruptible, sinless bodies. We will enter eternity without the ability or desire to sin and without the fear of death.

Read 1 Corinthians 15:55-57.

a. What is the sting of death?

b. How do we have victory over death?

16. As judgment comes to the wicked, we do not mourn (Isaiah 66:24). In order for death to be defeated, sin and those who practice it must be destroyed. We abhor their sins and rejoice that God and His people are finally vindicated.

a. Read Revelation 14:9-11.

What happens to those who worship the beast (the antichrist) and receive his mark?

b.  What is the smoke and for how long will it go up?

c.  Read Revelation 19:1-3.

What does the great multitude in heaven say when they see the smoke of the harlot?

Note:  The harlot is considered the idolatrous, false religions of the world. She is unfaithful to the Lord and teach doctrines of demons.

17.  What would heaven be like if sin and those who are still under the curse of sin were allowed to enter?

18.  Death is our enemy and it will be the last enemy destroyed when Jesus returns.

Read Isaiah 25:7-9.

a. What will God do for us when death is destroyed (v 8)?

b. After destroying death, God wipes away our tears. Never again will we mourn the loss of a loved one.

Will death ever be able to threaten God's people or His creation again? Explain.

After the wicked are judged and sentenced to eternal damnation in the lake of fire, death and Hades are also destroyed in the same manner. After God destroys death, He wipes away our tears. The sorrows of death are gone forever. We will forever praise God for defeating our enemy.

*The best moment of a Christian's life is his last one, because*

*it is the one that is nearest heaven. And then it is that he*

*begins to strike the keynote of the song which he shall sing to*

*all eternity.*

C.H. Spurgeon

# Week 8 - Declared from the Beginning

## Day 1 - New Heavens and New Earth

1. As a result of the Fall, all of God's creation fell under the curse of sin.

Read Isaiah 24:3-6.

What is the result of sin on planet earth?

2. Sin-cursed planet earth cannot last throughout eternity. The earth is in a state of decay and self-destruction. Similar to how believers will be resurrected and made new with incorruptible bodies, heaven and earth will be destroyed and made anew.

Read 2 Peter 3:10-13.

a. How will the current heaven and earth be destroyed?

b.  Throughout Scripture, the day of the Lord refers to Jesus' second coming.

When will the heaven and earth be destroyed (v 10)?

3.  Heaven and earth will be remade as perfect, eternal homes for their inhabitants.  The earth will never see corruption, weeds, or natural disasters.  Believers will dwell in the wonderful, new earth with our Lord.  God has no limits in His abilities.  Heaven and earth will not be restricted by their current size or existing laws of nature.  God can and will create whatever He pleases and it will be magnificent.  God has provided us insights into the hereafter that give us reasons to yearn for our new home.

Read Isaiah 65:17-19.

a.  What happens to our unbearable memories of this sin-cursed world?

b.  What will replace our distress and sadness?

4. Read 2 Peter 3:14, 17-18.

Knowing that this world and everything in it will be destroyed, how should we live?

5. The new heaven and earth will be vastly different than our current universe.

Read Revelation 21:1-11.

a. Where will God dwell (v 21:3)?

b. Why is there no more grief, sorrow or pain (v 21:4)?

c. Who will not inherit the eternal blessings of God (v 21:8)?

d. Finish this sentence from verse 21:7 (ESV).

The one who conquers will have this heritage,

_____.

While it is good to care for the planet and everything in it, we know from God's Word that this earth along with the entire universe will one day be destroyed. A new world is coming but not by human hands.

God will make all things new. He will create new heavens and a new earth that are incorruptible. The horrors of this sinful world will no longer haunt us. We will not need to search the universe for paradise, He's bringing paradise to us. Our minds cannot imagine the splendor of our eternal home.

*There are far, far better things ahead than any we leave behind.*

C. S. Lewis

6. When the earth and heaven are made new, time and seasons as we know them will cease to exist. Currently, weather patterns, tides, seasons and the calendar year (24 hour/day and night) are all controlled by the seas, moon and sun. With the new heaven and new earth comes new beginnings, including the natural laws of nature.

a. Read Psalm 104:19-20.

Why did God create the sun and moon?

b. Read Genesis 8:22.

How long will the four seasons last?

c. Read Revelation 21:23-25.

What happens to the current sun and moon?

d. Read Revelation 22:5.

What happens to the night?


e.  Read Revelation 21:1.


What happens to the sea?


7.  Death entered the world as a result of sin.  When sin and death are destroyed, we will no longer kill animals to eat, nor will animals attack and eat each other.


Read Isaiah 11:6-9.


How does this passage reflect the future harmony of nature?


8.  Since our new bodies will be incorruptible, we will not need food to sustain ourselves.  However, we may still eat for pleasure or other purposes.


Before His death, Jesus broke bread and shared wine with His disciples in the Upper Room.

Read Matthew 26:29.

What will Jesus again drink with His followers when He returns?

9.  Adam and Eve were kicked out of the Garden of Eden to prevent them from eating from the tree of life (as discussed in Week 1).  In the future, the tree of life is planted in the holy city, new Jerusalem.

Read Revelation 22:1-2 and 22:14.

a.  What benefit do the leaves from the tree of life provide?

b.  How many types of fruit will be on the tree of life?

c.  How many months will exist (consider the number of different fruits)?

Finally, everything will live in perfect harmony. While we will no longer experience sickness or death, the tree of life will have leaves that provide healing for the nations. Perhaps we will enjoy the comfort of the leaves as nourishment for our souls. The tree of life will also produce a different fruit for each of the 12 months. Considering that we will no longer have a 24-hour cycle of day and night, the calendar will be different than our current understanding. Time as we know it will no longer be necessary in eternity.

*I would not give one moment of heaven for all the joy and riches of the world, even if it lasted for thousands and thousands of years.*

Martin Luther

10. An inheritance is something that the recipient does not work to receive; it is a birth right or benefaction. Those who believe in Jesus Christ are born-again as heirs to His promises.

a. Read Psalm 33:12 and Galatians 3:29.

Who will receive His inheritance?

b. Read Romans 8:16-17.

What family relationship do we as believers have with God that makes us His heirs?

c. Read Romans 8:29.

Who is the first born among us?

d. Read Ephesians 1:5 and 1:11.

How does God bring us into His family as His sons and daughters?




e.  Read Hebrews 1:14.


What is our inheritance?




f.  Read 1 Peter 1:3-5.


How is our inheritance described in this passage?




11.  Our inheritance will bring us everlasting happiness as God makes all things right.


a.  Read Isaiah 51:11.


What will we receive when He returns?




b.  Read Matthew 5:3-12.

Write the future blessings of God next to each condition below.

Poor in spirit -

Meek -

Hunger and thirst for righteousness -

Merciful -

Pure in heart -

Peacemakers -

Persecuted for the Gospel -

God decided to adopt us as sons and daughters and make us heirs to His eternal kingdom. He created a family bond with us that cannot be broken. Not only will we inherit an incredible new earth, full of wonder, but we will also receive blessings of happiness and joy. We are so burdened in this life that our minds cannot comprehend the goodness that God has prepared for us. Overwhelming joy will fill our hearts and eternal optimism will be our attitude. We will be eternally satisfied, without want or need.

*In some ways, Christians are homeless. Our true home is waiting for us, prepared by the Lord Jesus Christ.*
Billy Graham

12. God is developing an eternal, family relationship with His people. God helps us understand our future relationship with Him through the illustration of a bride and her groom.

a. Read Isaiah 62:5 and Ephesians 5:25-27.

Who is the bride and how is she described?

b. Read John 1:29 and Revelation 21:9.

Who is the groom?

13. The bride includes all believers in Christ. The marriage ceremony is seen in John's vision after the second coming of Christ and before the millennium period.

a. Read Revelation 19:7-8.

Why are they rejoicing?

b.  Read Isaiah 61:10.

Where does the bride get her wedding garments and what do they represent?  (Also, consider Revelation 19:7-8 in your response.)

14.  As we previously discussed, our body and soul will be reunited when we are resurrected from the dead at Jesus' second coming.  Before His death, Jesus reassured His disciples that they would have a future home with Him.

Read John 14:1-3.

What is Jesus preparing for His followers?

15.  Jesus is preparing an eternal home for His bride.

a.  Read Revelation 21:1-11.

What is our new home called and where will it be located?

b. Review Revelation 21:22-24.

Why is there no temple in new Jerusalem?

c. Read Revelation 21:25.

Will the gates of the city ever close?

d. Review Revelation 22:14.

Who will be allowed to enter the holy city, new Jerusalem?

e. Read Revelation 22:15.

Who will forever be excluded from entering new Jerusalem?

God uses the bride and groom relationship to help us understand the intimate, everlasting relationship between Christ and His Bride - the Church.

God is the ultimate wedding planner; He provides both the bride and the groom. He prepares our wedding garments of salvation and righteousness through Jesus' work on the Cross.

At the wedding of the Lamb, the bride has made herself ready. She is dressed in white as she is presented to the groom in purity. The groom rejoices over His bride. He showers her with gifts as she shares in His inheritance.

All of heaven rejoices and is glad as the Father receives all the glory. God's predetermined plan from before the foundation of the world has been perfectly executed. He has prepared for Himself a people that He wants to spend eternity with. Jesus' love story with His bride is the true *happily ever after*.

*"I am my beloved's and my beloved is mine."*

Song of Solomon 6:3.

## *Day 5 - How Now Shall We Live?*

As we conclude this Bible study on Death and the Hereafter, let us take time to reflect on what God has taught us in His Word.

16.  Compared to when you started this study, how has your attitude toward death changed?  Explain.

17.  Do you feel more or less afraid of dying?  Explain.

18.  What areas in your life need to change so that you can become more eternally focused?

19. How does your attitude toward death impact your willingness to share the Gospel?

20. If someone were to ask you, "Why should I get saved?" How would you respond?

*Heaven is not a figment of imagination. It is not a feeling or an emotion. It is not the "Beautiful Isle of Somewhere." It is a prepared place for a prepared people.*

David Jeremiah

# Prayer of Repentance

If you are not ready for death, if Jesus is not the Lord of your life, then the prayer below is for you. Today is the day of salvation. Do not spend another minute in fear of death. Give your heart to Jesus so that you can live and die in peace.

*"Lord Jesus, I know that You are the Son of God and that You died on the cross for my sins. You did not stay dead but were raised from the dead on the third day. I am a sinner and deserving of Your righteous judgment. I know that I cannot save myself. I repent of my sins. Jesus, please come into my heart and be the Lord of my life. Give me a heart that seeks You and desires to do Your will. Give me a child-like faith. Thank You for forgiving me of my sins and for the gift of eternal life. Thank you for loving me and hearing my prayer. In Jesus' name I pray. Amen."*

*When we realize that God is the perfection of all that we long for or desire, that He is the summation of everything beautiful or desirable, then we realize that the greatest joy of the life to come will be that we "shall see His face."*

Wayne Grudem

For inquiries, email the author at

studythebiblewithkelly@gmail.com

Made in the USA
Columbia, SC
17 March 2021